BUILD YOUR OWN

BARREL OVEN

A GUIDE FOR MAKING A VERSATILE, EFFICIENT
AND EASY TO USE WOOD-FIRED OVEN

Max and Eva Edleson

Build Your Own Barrel Oven

A Guide for Making a Versatile, Efficient and Easy to Use Wood-Fired Oven

© Max and Eva Edleson 2012
www.firespeaking.com
info@firespeaking.com

Illustrations © 2012 Max Edleson
Photos © 2012 Eva Edleson, unless noted

Design & Layout by: Saritaksu Editions, Bali, Indonesia

Printed by Bang in the U.S.A.

All barrel ovens featured in this book were built by Max and Eva Edleson, except when noted. Thank you Elaine C. Johnson, Emi Miller, Sandor Katz and Kiko Denzer for help with editing this book.

ISBN: 978-0-9679846-9-8

Published by:

HAND PRINT PRESS
PO Box 576 Blodgett, OR 97326, USA
www.handprintpress.com

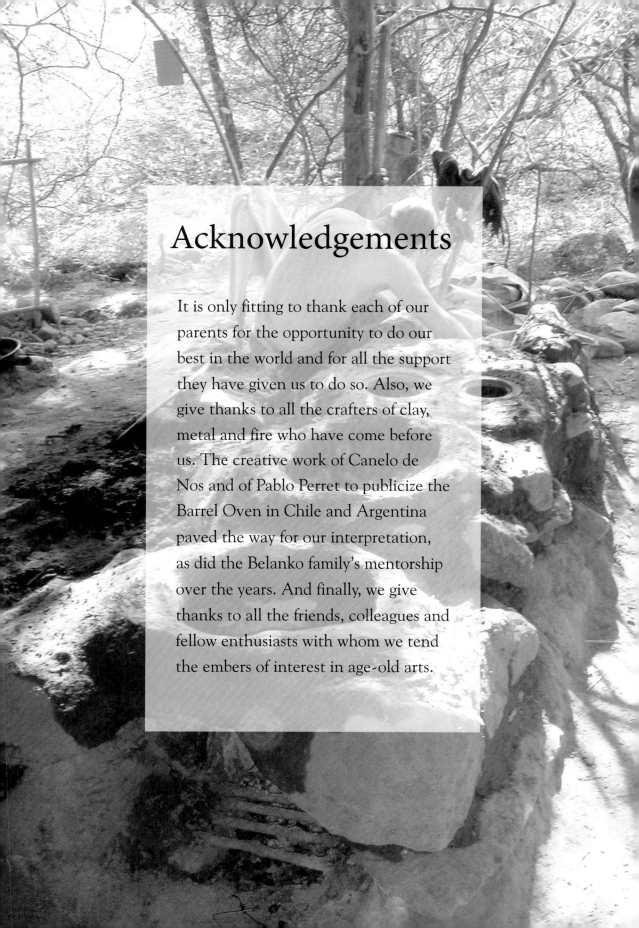

Acknowledgements

It is only fitting to thank each of our parents for the opportunity to do our best in the world and for all the support they have given us to do so. Also, we give thanks to all the crafters of clay, metal and fire who have come before us. The creative work of Canelo de Nos and of Pablo Perret to publicize the Barrel Oven in Chile and Argentina paved the way for our interpretation, as did the Belanko family's mentorship over the years. And finally, we give thanks to all the friends, colleagues and fellow enthusiasts with whom we tend the embers of interest in age-old arts.

Preface

Eva Edleson is a professional natural builder, cook, gardener, and craftswoman with over a decade of experience specializing in natural wall systems, wood-fired cooking and earthen paints and plasters. She has trained and worked with many of the most-respected natural builders in North America, as well as Argentina. Eva has combined her own research and experiences into a successful natural building practice.

My experience with Barrel Ovens began in October of 2007, I traveled to Argentina to visit my very good friend and now husband, Max Edleson. It was a very special time in my life, diving into crafts I had been studying and also learning new ones. During my visit, Max and I were invited to be a part of *Manos En La Tierra*, a gathering focused on permaculture and natural building classes.

We arrived early to be part of a small team that set up the infrastructure for the gathering. *Manos En La Tierra* was being held deep in rural Alijilan, Catamarca on a virgin piece of land surrounded by green and lush mountain forests. Our job was to create various facilities such as simple dwelling, bathing, cooking and dining areas for the 200 participants who would come. This is when I first became familiar with the Barrel Oven. Max had previously learned this style of baking oven from his friend and mentor Jorge Belanko, and we headed up the project to provide a barrel oven for the gathering.

This Barrel Oven cost us nothing to build. It was created completely from the natural landscape surrounding us and a few things that we scavenged at the nearest dump. We gathered stones from the land to build the body of the oven and sifted the clay rich soil for mortar. The shelves for the oven were fashioned out of an old bedspring and the chimney was built with stone. As we built the Barrel Oven in the growing kitchen, a man named Al constructed "The Train" – a long earthen tunnel designed to cook three pots of ingredients simultaneously. The Train was also a wood-fired cooking device and included a griddle in the back for making chapatis. I was very impressed with how one fire at the front of the stove could be channeled to cook so many dishes at once.

Though I had been studying natural building for years prior to this gathering, and had built multiple earthen ovens, this was the first Barrel Oven that I had ever made. As a cook, I appreciated how fast the Barrel Oven was able to reach baking temperatures as well as its large and flexible capacity.

The simplicity of building something that is both functional and enduring with what you have easily at hand is so deeply satisfying. Within a week we were baking loaves of bread, rice casseroles, roasted vegetables, and able to nicely prepare delicious meals that fed the entire group of participants.

I am convinced that making our shelter, building our ovens and growing our food gives us a powerful sense of dignity, joy and pride. This is especially true when the result of our labor is beautiful, useful and comfortable. I believe that the desire for this connection is strong within us all and encourage everyone to engage in the process of making things using simple materials and time-tested techniques.

We offer this book as a way to document our experience and share with you the steps of how you can build your own. We hope that you will build your Barrel Oven and enjoy the many delicious and nourishing meals that you will proudly share with your family and friends.

- Eva Rose Edleson January 2012

(Middle photo, Jonathan Shaw, Bottom Photo, Max Livingstone)

Max is a professional artist/ builder who is dedicated to using naturally and locally available materials to create energy-efficient and spiritually-uplifting elements of homes and public spaces. Masonry heaters and wood-fired ovens are the main focus of his work, along with reviving the practice of using wood as a sustainable fuel to meet basic cooking and heating needs. Max combines these professional activities with a passion for farming, homesteading, and other traditional crafts.

I came across the Barrel Oven during my first days in Argentina. There was one built with a simple roof over it at the Center for Sustainable Agriculture (CIESA) where I had gone to apprentice. I had been studying bread baking for a number of years and immediately realized the utility of the Barrel Oven. It was responsive, easy to use and met all my criteria for simple and useful solutions that improve life without damaging the earth or hurting other people. The wood-fired aspect enchanted me as I was only getting to know wood as a fuel at that time.

It was also a significant historical moment in Argentina. The country experienced the largest economic crisis that a "modern" developed economy has experienced. There was almost no cash in circulation and the barter economies based on locally printed currencies had become a primary field for many people's activities. Along with the vegetables that I would bring to sell, it was always so satisfying to make large batches of granola in our Barrel Oven to take to the market. Several other families I knew sold things made in their Barrel Ovens.

My interest in farming grew into an interest in sustainable shelter and from there into sustainable ways to cook and heat our homes. I perceived that there was a lack of expertise in this area and proceeded to delve deeper into this subject which has now become a central focus of my work. Among the early projects, my brother and I built a Barrel Oven in our home in which we baked bread weekly and used to cook many meals. Seven years later, it is still producing bread every week.

The many happy experiences that Eva and I had in Argentina both baking in and building this style of oven were inspirations for this book. We wanted to make this information available in English since we have found that there is little coverage for this pattern of building for fire.

We continue to be interested in wood as a fuel for heating and cooking because of its tangible proximity, abundance and regenerative capacity. At the same time, news and information about other mainstream fuel sources (such as nuclear, oil, electricity, and liquid natural gas) are often conflicting and uncertain with regards to their ecological effects, social impact and long-term dependability. There does not appear, however, to be much public support through university research or grants for ways of making wood more efficient, cleaner and easier to use as a fuel source for domestic use. The quest has been taken on mostly by tinkerers, do-it-yourselfers, and brave professionals who assume the risks and rewards of innovation in their work. The Barrel Oven is one emerging pattern that we have dedicated a great deal of energy towards over the last 5 years.

This book, therefore, is a summary of research and a synthesis of experience. There is still vast room for improvement of this design. We hope that this printing will accelerate the collective process of investigation and refinement which leads to the strengthening of our traditions. It would make our wish for the book come true if people picked it up, put it down, built ovens that fed families and baked in them to supplement their incomes. We also hope that many good and better ideas come along and that we may continue to be a part of the conversation.

May this book play a humble role in providing yet another option for combining the old and the new into a vessel for receiving nature's miraculous gifts.

- Max Edleson January 2012

What is a Barrel Oven?

A Barrel Oven is a versatile wood-fired oven that is relatively easy to build and easy to use. It can be the seed for a small-scale baking enterprise or the heart of a community's wood-fired cuisine. All kinds of food can be baked in the Barrel Oven including bread, roasts, pizza, cookies, cakes, pies, casseroles and stews.

The Barrel Oven offers surprising convenience because it is hot and ready to bake in within 15-20 minutes of lighting a fire. Another great feature is that it is easy to maintain at a desired temperature for long periods of time. This type of oven is often called a "mixed oven" because it has the capability to cook with direct as well as stored heat.

The Barrel Oven can be built almost entirely out of recycled, re-sourced and local materials. It can also be made with brand new, manufactured and bought parts. At its center is a metal barrel, of which there are many in the waste-stream. One or more racks to bake on are constructed inside and a door is fashioned at one end. Wood-fired cooking enthusiasts appreciate the capacity that two deep shelves offer, allowing the ability to bake eight to ten 2 lb (1 kg) loaves of bread, four 12" (30 cm) pizzas or four cookie sheets at a time.

When cooking in the Barrel Oven, a fire is built in the firebox located beneath the barrel. The fire hits the bottom and wraps tightly around the barrel as it travels through the carefully constructed space between the metal barrel and the surrounding bricks. This extended contact between the fire and the metal concentrates the heat for cooking inside the barrel and is what allows the

Barrel Oven to heat up so fast.

Building a Barrel Oven is a manageable project for experienced builders as well as people new to construction. It is very satisfying to begin with nothing and then create something which becomes a gathering place for good meals and good times. It is also ideal for those exploring natural building as it offers experiences building a foundation, making and laying your own bricks, and constructing a simple roof structure - all on a comfortable scale.

The Barrel Oven, as presented here, is a very simple pattern which can be modified and varied to improve the cooking experience. There is great potential also to adapt this pattern into hybrid wood-fired heating and cooking designs. The art of constructing a Barrel Oven includes many possible materials such as brick, stone, adobe, compressed earth blocks, and cob. We present variations in use of materials as well as design, and offer this book as a jumping-off point into further experimentation that will surely lead to improvements.

A Barrel Oven made with red brick and finished with an earthen plaster. (Photo, June Bonnheim)

Mother and daughter share the joy of pulling a pizza out of an oven they built.

Is the Barrel Oven for You?

A Comparison of Oven Options

Lighting a fire is an important part of the ritual of cooking in a Barrel Oven.

Wood-fired bake ovens have experienced a real resurgence in popularity in many parts of the world. For some, this comes from an interest in taste and tradition, and for others from exploring resilience in communities and an emphasis on using and preserving local resources. Cooking with wood imbues food with a special quality. In direct-fired ovens, part of this comes from the unique smoky taste and the occasional mixing of ash with the food. Even in wood-fired cooking methods where the fire and the cooking surface are separate, such as in Barrel Ovens, the time and care necessary to harvest and prepare the wood as well as the connected process of tending a fire through the cooking process is present in the tastes the food develops.

Choosing to build and use a Barrel Oven is one option among many for creating a productive baking tool. People interested in a Barrel Oven may or may not already have a gas or electric oven, so the wood-fired oven can either be complementary or provide new baking possibilities. Oftentimes the choice being made is between the Barrel Oven and the more traditionally known dome or vaulted wood-fired ovens.

The most well-known wood-fired ovens are direct-fired and have enough mass in their walls to store the heat from the fire, and then later radiate it back to the food, even after the fire and any coals have been removed. The shapes of these ovens are often either domed or vaulted. They can be sculpted with earth or constructed with earthen or fired brick. They can be large or small, and can vary greatly, accommodating budgets of almost nothing up to the cost of buying or building an entire house.

It can sometimes be a difficult decision to determine what kind of oven is most suitable for you, so we will do our best to share our own personal experience as well as experience gleaned from talking to others in the process of making this same decision. Thinking about wood-fired ovens along a spectrum of many options, the Barrel Oven falls somewhere in the middle.

If you are looking for a wood-fired oven that you use occasionally to bake in, especially when you have guests or want to make a special meal for your family, then a smaller brick or earthen oven is a good choice. These ovens are celebratory and add the spark and fun of fire to our lives. When cooking in these ovens, you make the fire directly inside the oven. Smaller ovens usually require a 2-3 hour fire to heat the mass up sufficiently for baking. You then remove the coals and clean the oven before baking in it. Dishes requiring different temperatures can then be cooked over a period of time as the stored heat decreases.

The Barrel Oven is great for people who are interested in baking more often and for those who are likely to want to use wood as a primary fuel source. The Barrel Oven is a highly functional

Cooking in the Barrel Oven is a fun thing to do with friends and family. (Top photo, April Magill)

and efficient wood-fired oven. Its much shorter pre-heating period (15-20 minutes) to arrive at baking temperature works well for people with busy schedules and those who may not be able to plan exactly when they will need to start baking. The large capacity offered by the two shelves, and the ease with which one can maintain a baking temperature over a long period, makes volume baking possible– although it certainly also shines when you want to cook a small meal spontaneously! Since ash and carbon are not introduced to the cooking chamber, it is always clean and you can use baking sheets and pans interchangeably with another kind of oven. The element of fire does tend to be more contained in the Barrel Oven and the wood-fired "smoky" taste is not present in the food cooked in it. In general, we consider the Barrel Oven a practical "work-horse" wood-fired oven that is efficient in its use of wood and easy to use.

Interestingly, as you go up in size, larger earthen and brick ovens can return to being the most efficient option. These ovens use wood most efficiently when they are used regularly and maintained at a constant temperature, especially when they are well insulated. This is the case for traditional village ovens and is also the case for dedicated commercial bakeries. In this situation, a good portion of the wood's energy is not used to get up to temperature (and lost in cooling down) but rather used to maintain temperature over long periods of time.

Given the minimal investment and high productivity that the Barrel Oven provides, we are confident that this style of oven will become more popular as awareness about it grows.

"...the Barrel Oven (is) a practical "work-horse" wood-fired oven... efficient in its use of wood and easy to use."

Choosing a Site

It is important to think of where you will place the oven in relation to the flows of activities that happen around it.

Outdoor Barrel Oven kitchen design with counter tops and room for sitting. Notice roofing which allows for a central firepit.

Consider combining multiple cooking systems. Here a wood-fired griddle complements this Barrel Oven. A stone counter top was later placed to connect the two.

Small outdoor kitchen area (in construction), including prep and serving counters, room for wood storage and a number of friends! Shelter by Casey Slezak.

A Barrel Oven built into the wall of a community kitchen with the addition of a wood-fired cookstove. (Oven built by CIDEP, Patagonia, Argentina)

Ovens tend to be gathering places... whether to stand around together to wait for pizzas to come out or to inquire curiously about what is creating those amazing wafts of cookie-scented temptation.

We enjoy for an oven to have a nice social space around it so that we can be attentive to what's cooking in it while hanging out with friends. You don't want to be leaving the main stage of a fun dinner party every couple of minutes to stoke the fire and check on your food. **Make the area around the oven a gathering place so that you can both tend to the cooking and participate in the entertainment.**

The easier it is for you to engage with your oven, the more likely it is you will use it. Consider how the location of the oven relates to the places that food is made and served. Imagine the path and process of carrying baking sheets of carefully risen bread or heavy pans of lasagna from where they are prepared to the hot oven that awaits them. **Since most Barrel Ovens are built outdoors, it is a good choice to locate yours where it has easy access to your indoor kitchen.**

We encourage including counter-tops into outdoor kitchen designs because they are essential tools for food preparation and service. Another important relationship exists between the oven and where you will be storing your firewood. **Design storage for some firewood right next to the oven, and plan the pathway to your main wood storage.**

Take some time to think through, and even act out, the various steps of prepping, cooking and serving. Acting out these processes will help you immensely in coming up with a successful design that integrates these new elements into the other aspects of your life. Do you want to have benches or tables set up nearby? Will it be comfortable and enjoyable year-round? Do you want a sink as part of your kitchen? If so, is there existing plumbing that you can connect to? And where will your sink drainage go? Can you water a nearby garden with the greywater?

The Importance of a Roof

In practice, the area that you create is defined by the area covered and protected by a roof. **It is essential that the oven have a roof over it.** The roof will protect the oven, keep it dry, and offer a place to cook in rainy weather. Make sure the roofed area not only protects the oven, but also protects at least the cook using the oven. We recommend also covering enough space for a small gathering of people. **It is important to think about how you will roof the oven as you plan the oven's location and construction.**

This Barrel Oven shelter design features a built-in counter, room for wood storage, and cover enough for the baker.

Basic Design Recommendations

A few basic recommendations for the creation of an oven and surrounding area.
1) Create a small, independent roof structure to

house the oven, which could also include one or more work counters, a sink, benches and a place to store wood.

Example:

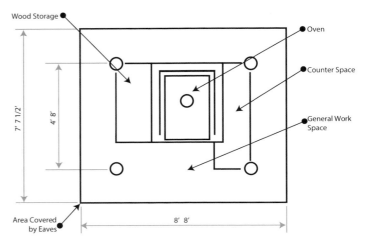

2) Locate the oven so that the firebox and oven door are part of an indoor kitchen wall and most of the body of the oven is protected by a simple shed roof on the outside of the building. This enables you to use your oven from within your building and you don't have to take up valuable interior space with the volume of an oven.

3) Create a small building for the oven which functions as a bakery or restaurant with space for storing supplies/ingredients, work counters, a sink, proofing shelves, and wood storage.

Often projects develop over time. You might begin with your oven and then later add benches and a sink. Spend some time dreaming about how the oven will be used in years to come. Your Barrel Oven could easily last for many generations.

The face of a Barrel Oven can be built inside a building while the bulk of its body and the chimney remain outside.

Materials

In this book, we present photos sharing the process of how several different Barrel Ovens were built. You will see that the resources and materials used vary significantly although they all follow the same basic pattern. Our best recommendation for choosing materials is to opt, whenever possible, for those that inspire you and that are locally available.

The Barrel and Other Metal Parts

The barrel is obviously one of the most important components of your oven. It is what separates the food from the fire and smoke while at the same time transmitting a good deal of its heat.

We look for the thickest gauge metal barrels we can find. They are usually 55-gallon (200 L) barrels although we also like smaller barrels with similar proportions since this size can work well for a small family or smaller baking loads.

The best metal barrels are the ones used to transport food products like honey or strawberry preserves. These are often available from local health food stores or other restaurant-related businesses. The food-grade barrels are thick and have removable lids which allows for making a well-sealed door.

Stripping the barrel of paint and any other residues is an important and somewhat messy step. We make a sizable hot fire and expose all the surfaces, especially the inside ones, to high heat so the paint burns completely off. We also sometimes use steel wool (and flexible paint cleaning attachments for electric drills) to finish cleaning the inside of the barrel. Make sure to wear a good quality dust-mask or respirator! Burning the barrel to remove paint is a low-tech solution which may only be viable in rural situations and is not the healthiest of processes.

Similar techniques are used for preparing barrels

Choose materials that inspire you and that are local.

Thick gauge metal barrels, stripped of all paint and residues. (Photo, Dylan Boye)

Part of the fun is using what you can find. Here, our friend makes an oven rack from an old bedframe.

Cooking in a Barrel Oven is very similar to cooking in an electric or gas oven. Here you see pizzas going in the oven! (Using pizza "stones" improves the quality of the crust.)

for rocket mass heaters. We have also used blow torches and grinders for cleaning rocket mass heater barrels but they don't work for preparing Barrel Ovens because it is difficult to clean the inside with these tools.

We were happy to discover a company called Industrial Container Services (www.iconserv.com) that specializes in re-branding metal barrels. (This company has locations throughout the U.S. and there may be similar companies in other locales.) They burn barrels in kilns at a very high temperature and then sandblast them. The barrels and lids we get from them have been restored to their original metal. We feel confident about both the hygiene of using these well-cleaned barrels, as well as the trouble and health hazards we avoid in not having to process the barrels ourselves. Even though we like to craft things from scratch, this is one step we are happy to forego.

The minimum amount of metal work necessary for a Barrel Oven is to fashion at least one rack on which to place baked goods, and a door with a latch which provides a tight seal to keep the heat in when closed. This work can be done using simple hand tools including a drill, and nuts and bolts for attachment between metal pieces.

We make our ovens with a system of two racks and two removable shelves. The ability to remove the top shelf is important when you want to bake larger items such as whole-animal roasts, large pumpkins, and big stew pots! We also fabricate an insulated door that keeps the heat inside. The door's hinges are weighted so the door stays closed without requiring a latch. The racks inside the oven are bolted to the barrel so that they can be removed and installed in another barrel if the original one ever burns out. We use a welder and a grinder to do a lot of this work.

The Barrel Oven kit from Firespeaking. We proudly make all these parts from raw steel stock in our workshop. We then finish visible surfaces with high temperature stove paint.

You can either do this metal work yourself or find a local metal worker to help or do it for you. You can also order the fabricated barrel or the whole kit from us at **www.firespeaking.com**.
See also Appendix 2: Obtaining a Barrel Oven Kit.

A Body of Brick and Stone

The noble materials listed on the next page generally can be considered to have the properties of thermal mass. They serve both as a fire-resistant shape that focuses heat directly into the barrel, as well as a battery that stores the heat and radiates it back over time. This dual function explains why the Barrel Oven is often called a "mixed" oven in South America.

A comparison of common building blocks:

Fired brick is durable and convenient but can be hard to cut and shape.

Adobe bricks are easy to cut and shape and can be made from the earth beneath your feet. They do require energy and time to make and can vary

Homemade adobe bricks offer the opportunity to build with local materials and have fun! This is a great community activity.

in quality depending on materials and technique. We highly recommend watching the educational DVD *Mud, Hands, A House* to learn how to make adobe bricks (and many other earthen building techniques!).

Stone can be sourced locally. Stone takes more time to lay, can be difficult to cut and shape, and is often enchanting in appearance. Some stones hold up to heat and direct flame better than others. Consider using brick to construct the firebox.

Cob is a hand-sculpted earthen material made from clay, sand and straw. It is intuitive. It is also slower because it requires load-bearing parts to harden significantly before continuing.

Mortars

Mortars can be made from clay, cement and/or lime mixed with sand. These first ingredients act as binders and the sand gives grit and structure to the mix. Without going into depth on a subject that is an art unto itself, suffice it to say that using three parts sand to one part of some combination of these binders should work. Our preference is to make and use clay-based mortars. They are easier on our bodies; it is easier to keep our work and our tools clean, and using a softer mortar preserves the masonry units so that they can be re-used in other configurations centuries later. The one significant drawback is that clay-based mortars require a roof.

Common red brick are great to build with and easy to find, often for free. Mortar made from clay and sand is enjoyable to apply by hand.

Chimney

A chimney is an essential part of the Barrel Oven's design and function. It helps to create draft, which encourages a healthy fire, and channels smoke up and away from the oven, your workspace, and your guests. It is essential to plan the chimney from the earliest stage, as its connection through a roof (or out a wall) is necessary for a successful oven.

There are many options for chimney materials. For example; you can use stainless steel, steel (painted black), galvanized metal, stone, ceramic flue tiles, sculpted cob, and corrugated roofing. Even old tin cans would do in a pinch.

A 5" (13 cm) diameter pipe is ideal, although 6" (15 cm) stovepipe is often easier to source and will also work. We've found that 5-6' (1 ½ - 2 m) of height provides the oven with sufficient draw. The height of the roof protecting the oven will also be a factor in determining your chimney height. Single wall pipe is sufficient though you might choose/need to use double wall pipe and flashing where the chimney connects through the roof.

We place a chimney cap at the top of the pipe,

A good chimney installation is very important for function and safety. Don't hesitate to ask for help with this task from people who have experience.

Lighting, wood-storage, counter-tops and places to hang oven tools are important parts of functional kitchen desgin.

which sometimes comes with spark arresters (some kind of mesh to protect the release of flying embers) or sometimes we make our own.

Chimneys are both simple and complex and it is important to be very conscientious about your chimney installation for safety and function. Be especially careful in any places where the chimney is close to flammable materials such as wood. Do not hesitate to seek help or advice.

A chimney is an essential part of the Barrel Oven's design and function. It helps to create draft, which encourages a healthy fire, and channels smoke up and away from the oven, your workspace, and your guests.

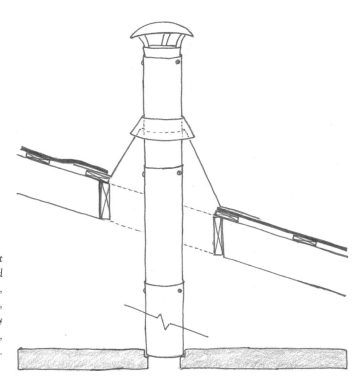

Tools

A suggested list .... tools required on depend on your project...

3-5	Buckets
1	Wheelbarrow
2	Shovels
1	Mortar Board, Pan or Tub
1	Machete or Brick Hammer
2-3	Levels (2', 4', and small speed level/1')
1	Small Sledgehammer
1	Cold Chisel
2-3	Diamond shaped trowels for cement and mortar work
1	Hacksaw or 4 ½" Grinder w/ masonry (diamond) and metal cutting disks
1	Eye and Ear Protection
1+	Sponges/Cleaning Brushes, Rags

If you are making your own metal parts for your Barrel Oven, you will need to use additional tools. They may include a manual or electric drill and welding equipment.

This Barrel Oven was built with on-site materials: stones and clay-rich soil. Flexible branches were used for the arch form. (Photo, Max Edleson)

In preparing for this book, we tried hard to develop a model with specific plans for standard units that we imagined would be available at hardware stores and masonry suppliers. As we realized that barrel sizes varied and even what we thought were standard brick sizes vary, we were reminded how important it is to, above all, pay attention and work with the materials that are available to us rather than forcing any sort of strict prescription. This happens in our work all the time and it is when we appreciate having developed an intuitive sculptor's understanding of the shapes involved rather than an overly precise and inflexible plan for action.

The Build/Construction

We revel in the fact that each construction project is unique. No matter how much any builder wants to copy a plan, what he or she creates is unique to the exact time, place and the materials available for construction. Use good judgment, ask experienced people for help and be confident in the fact that you are creating something new!

For these reasons, our construction instructions provide a basic model, like a sculptor's sketch, for you to follow in creating your Barrel Oven. Barrel sizes and especially brick sizes vary greatly so it is important to have the actual materials you will work with before getting too specific. For planning purposes, you can use a rough footprint of 38" wide x 42" deep (1m x 1.2m) to lay out a basic Barrel Oven in the context of other things in the planned space.

As you build, think about the dishes you will cook and the many great times ahead! Check in with your layout as you build. Always check for square, plumb and level.

Layout and Template

The layout of the oven is based on the size of the metal drum you will be using and the size of brick you have at hand.

Start by drawing on paper your specific Barrel Oven layout. Begin with the dimensions of your barrel and work out from there including the width of the airspace and the width of your bricks. We generally use a 2" air space surrounding the sides of the barrel and a ½" air space in the back. Notice that the front and back are not symmetrical. The barrel needs to overlap the front brick by at least half the brick's width for support.

Next, transfer your layout measurements in full scale onto cardboard or scrap plywood. This will be a useful template throughout construction. It is helpful to include details of the dimensions, locations and markings for the foundation, base, stone or brick, ash drawer, firebox door, location of the chimney and details like space for your plaster.

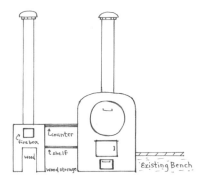

There are so many ways that the Barrel Oven can fit into a design. It often goes well with other cooking devices such as the griddle shown above. What will be most beautiful and enjoyable for you? (Illustration, Eva Edleson)

Transfer your layout measurements in full scale onto cardboard or scrap plywood. This gives you a comprehensive view of the project which you can refer to and helps you to understand how your materials will fit together.

This process gives you a comprehensive view of the project which you can refer to and helps you to understand how your materials will fit together.

Think through and sketch out the various components that you will use. This will help you to fine-tune your project. We also find it is very helpful to lay out the materials you will be using so that you can get a clear idea of how all of the components will relate to each other.

One great example of how useful a template can be is its role in determining the exact location to build the oven when planning a chimney which will exit between two existing rafters. You can drop a plumb-bob from between the two rafters and move the full-scale template into place so that its center on the ground aligns with the correct location up on the roof.

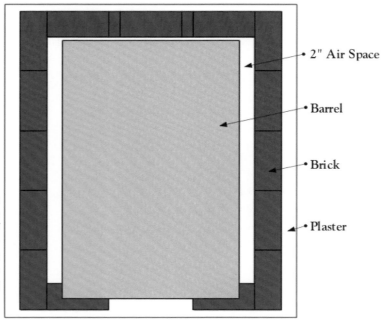

2" Air Space

Barrel

Brick

Plaster

Determine a specific brick layout which uses as many full bricks as possible to minimize cuts. If you are planning to plaster your oven, make sure to consider this thickness in your layout. Here is one example of a layout drawing that includes room for a thick, insulative plaster layer.

Vertical cross section

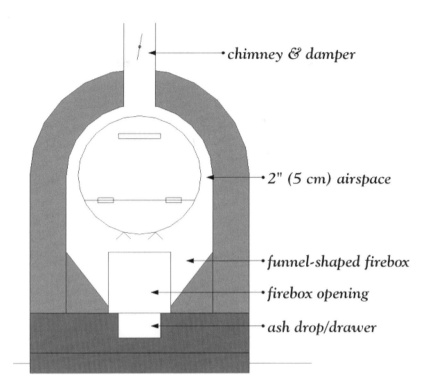

- chimney & damper
- 2" (5 cm) airspace
- funnel-shaped firebox
- firebox opening
- ash drop/drawer

It is helpful to draw a vertical cross section of the Barrel Oven. This process will help you understand the construction process and allow you to anticipate strategies at specific points, along with materials that you might need. It will help you know, for example, the approximate finished height of your oven so you can plan the roof.

Foundation

A foundation gives you a stable base for your oven. The process we outline here involves first addressing drainage, digging down to stable ground, and then filling with tamped gravel to establish a good base.

Before beginning work on your foundation, it is essential to prepare the overall site and think about drainage. Anticipate how water will move through your site. Flatten the area where the Barrel Oven will be built and ensure that there is a slight slope away

Make sure you are building on good solid ground. Digging and filling with rock below grade provides drainage and stability.

Friends and family who built the Barrel Oven together gather under the roof, awaiting the delicious meal cooking within. (Photo, June Bonnheim)

> *"A foundation gives you a stable base for your oven...."*

from the oven in each direction so that water will move away from it. It is important to do any of this kind of surface grading before digging.

Once you have chosen and cleared the site, transfer the perimeter of the template onto the ground. This will represent the footprint of your oven. We dig a footprint 2-3" wider than our template. You can "draw" it on the ground by using a flat shovel to mark the shape of the template.

We generally work in mild, temperate climates so we find that digging down about a foot usually gets us down to compact, undisturbed subsoil. In areas with deep frost, you might choose to dig deeper. Once you have dug down to your chosen depth, tamp the bottom of the trench well.

We then fill the foundation with "round fill rock" or "river rock" (about 1 ½" size), which is firmly tamped along the way. The roundish rock leaves space for good drainage. Be sure to stop filling with this drain rock 3-5" below grade so that the pad or the first layer of foundation stone ends up being half-embedded by what surrounds it.

Bear in mind, there are many alternatives to this

method. It would probably also work just fine to remove the organic layer of soil, tamp, lay a level of cinder block and start building on top of that. It all depends on the resources that you have at hand and level of perfection and longevity you are looking for.

Pad

Next, we recommend building a "pad" which provides connection and continuity at the base.

While concrete has become the norm for foundations, it is rewarding to explore alternatives such as stone, urbanite (recycled concrete), or other repurposed materials. An existing concrete slab, patio or driveway can also serve as a pad for your Barrel Oven.

The pad should be the size of your template and made of units that are as wide as possible, (sometimes done as one piece). This will unify the load of the smaller bricks that you will place above. Ensure that your pad is square by checking that your diagonals measure equally.

Make sure that the pad is nestled partly above and partly below grade to ensure that it will not slide in the event of earth movement. **It is essential that it is level** and that it does not move in any direction.

A pad provides connetion, continuity, and unifies the load of the oven on the base. Make yours out of urbanite, concrete blocks, gravel bags or pour your own concrete pad.

Material options for the pad:

Urbanite - (aka recycled concrete) Must be well placed and snug. Use small round fill rock and/or sand to pack in between the pieces of urbanite.

Concrete - Pour a concrete pad by using boards to make the form and reinforce with rebar.

Solid Concrete Blocks or Cinder blocks - Use mostly whole, some halves.
Gravel Bags - Another option for the pad is to use polypropylene bags filled with gravel (similar to earthbag construction).

Ash Drawer

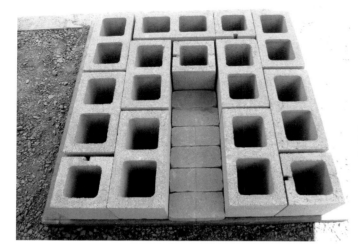

Space cinder blocks to the specific dimensions of your materials.

The next step is to build a space to collect the ash that accumulates from firing your oven. It needs to be easily accessible so that you can remove the ash from time to time.

The simplest way is to simply build a long, relatively narrow cavity.

In our Barrel Oven Kit, we have designed an ash drawer that slides snugly in this space for easy removal of the ash. The way the front of the ash drawer constrains the amount of air coming in means that the ash drawer doubles as an air register.

Note: If you are going to build your Barrel Oven using earthen materials, you will still need to build the ash area out of stone, brick, block, or urbanite. This base will raise the earthen materials off the ground, protecting them from moisture and preventing water from rising by capillary action into the walls. This ensures durability and good performance.

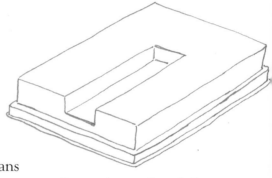

Create a place to collect ash. If using a drawer, it can double as an air register.

Grate

Next comes the construction of the grate which has a surprisingly important role in the health of the fire and ease of use in the oven. The grate sits upon the space for the ash collection you have created. We recommend using a simple welded grate. Alternatives include tying individual pieces of re-bar with wire to pieces that run the full length or finding a sturdy piece of metal with regularly spaced holes which can serve as a grate.

Think about creating just enough space, ¼-⅜" (½ - 1cm) for the ash to fall through, but only enough

The grate sits upon the ash space you have created. Here you can see a durable grate and firebox door made by Firespeaking.

Though you can use recycled pieces of metal and embed them in cob, we have found that this is not so durable over time.

space so that smaller embers and the rest of the fire are held up well. We use ½" (12mm) rebar which seems to be sufficiently sturdy for repeated long-term use; ⅜" (10mm) rebar would probably work fine too. We look forward to hearing about other creative solutions that people come up with.

Reflections on the Role of Grates for Fire by Max

Following the instructions in Spanish that we originally had, we used to simply mortar or cob in many similar lengths of ½" rebar to create the grate. We found that over time these lengths had a way of working themselves out of the mortar, a result of repeated expansion and contraction the metal experiences as it heats and cools, and the mechanical wear this area experiences as wood is thrown in and re-arranged under hurried, hot conditions.

In the Rio Azul oven, it was through the displacement of the bars in the grate, the resulting holes that developed and its negative impact on the fire that I was able to learn a lot about the role of the grate and the importance of the formation and maintenance of embers in the health of a fire. The holes from the missing lengths of rebar caused large embers to drop from the core of the fire into the ash box. This made it much harder to maintain a good fire because the fire's "heart", the good formation of a central hot collection of embers, kept dropping out of its center.

I was interested in how this situation might be remedied. I wasn't convinced that re-mortaring the missing pieces of rebar would be a very durable solution. Most of the other pieces of rebar weren't really mortared in anymore anyway but rather precariously placed across the bricks that created the space for the ashes. Given the remote location of the Rio Azul oven, a spool of wire was as close as we were going to get to welding metal. So I removed all the bars, cut two lengths that would go perpendicular to them along the length of the grate, and tightly tied each piece to these cross pieces. Alex, who uses that stove regularly, has reported that the simple baling wire solution has endured perfectly for three years now.

Building the Firebox and Outside Walls

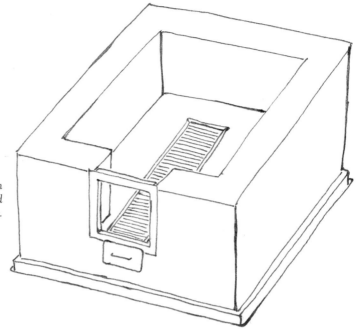

The outside walls give definition to the volume of the oven and contain the firebox.

The funnel-shaped firebox helps to keep the fire organized over the grate.

The next task is to create the funnel-shaped firebox. To do so, you must build the outside walls first in order to rest the diagonally-placed bricks of the firebox against them. This shape helps to keep the fire organized, burning well, and concentrated over the grate, and begins the sculptural form that will take the heated gases up and tightly around the barrel.

Make a dry layout of the first course of the firebox making sure to leave the space for your door opening. When you are satisfied with your layout, mortar the bricks in place and continue with the next courses.

Once the outside walls are high enough you will lay an entire course of bricks diagonally on either side of the grate (and toward the back). Mortar all points of contact and fill the triangular spaces behind each brick with sand, clay and sand, rocks and clay, or perlite and clay, etc. Fill well to create solid support for the bricks.

The Firebox Door and Lintel

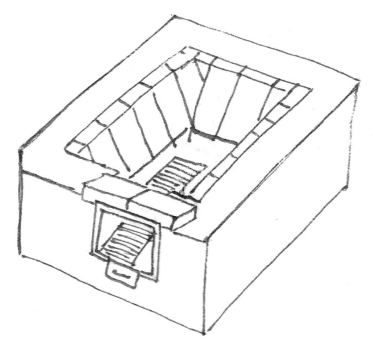

The funnel-shaped firebox keeps the fire organized, burning well, and concentrated over the grate.

Although brick sizes vary, you'll want to plan for the top of a course of brick to coincide with the top of your firebox. This will enable you to place a lintel across the firebox opening at the right height. It usually works out to reach the top of the firebox with either three or four courses of brick (depending on whether you are using larger adobes or smaller fired brick).

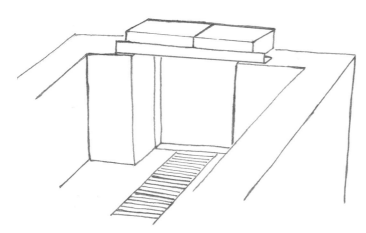

This drawing shows one example of how to span across the firebox door by using angle iron. Another option is to build an arch here.

Plan for the top course of brick to coincide with the top of the firebox. This will enable you to place a lintel across the firebox opening at the right height.

Plan your mortar joint spacing and get it right, especially if you are building for pre-made hardware.

We generally place a lintel across the top of the firebox door or opening with an angle iron and place a single course of brick on the lintel to span across. This creates a platform that supports the barrel that will be placed above it. When building with adobe, we often use fired brick here because it is a place that is both structurally important and which experiences significant thermal and physical wear.

Different Rates of Expansion & How to Accommodate for This

It is important to know that metal expands significantly more than masonry when heated. Understanding this is crucial to success in building for fire when combining these complementary but very different materials.

When using angle iron as a lintel, for example, mortar bricks only to themselves and not to the metal. Before the mortar at either end of the lintel has set up, tap the angle iron so that it moves a ¼"- ½" (0.5 cm-1 cm) in either direction along its length. This will provide space which acts as an expansion gap and will reduce the probability of cracking.

Another technique is to place ceramic wool or layers of scrunched aluminum foil to act as an expansion buffer between the two materials. You can see this in the photographic examples around the firebox door and also around the barrel. High temperature silicone is also an option for this application.

Another good option is to skip the problems having to do with embedded metal altogether and build an arch. This is a good option, especially for a simple Barrel Oven that does not use any metal work for the firebox opening. In this case, the opening should not be too wide in order to limit the amount of air that enters the firebox. Many a simple Barrel Oven has an old baking tray or other sheet of metal that serves as a door.

Supporting the Barrel

You are ready to place supports from front to back to support the barrel. We usually do this by using two pieces of 1 ½" x ³/₁₆" angle iron. Pipe and other strong pieces of metal can also work.

Make sure that the supports are centered on the front and back, and that they are level. Shim

The barrel is supported by two pieces of angle iron. It is also possible to support the barrel directly on the front and back walls. Here the supports are shown after the completion of the arch.

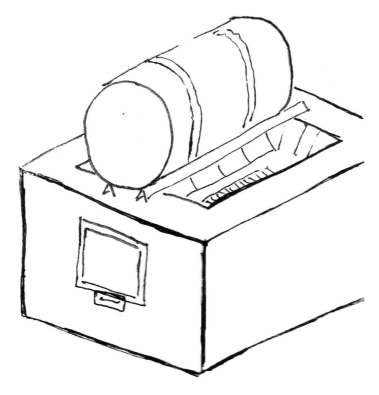

carefully with pieces of brick or rock if you have to. Secure supports in place with a stiff mix of clay and sand or other mortar.

Place the actual barrel on at this point and check that the cooking shelves are level in all directions. You don't want your delicious tray of caramel custard to gravitate to one side of the dish because you didn't get this step right.

It is important to spend time making sure that the cooking shelves are level in all directions while leveling and permanently fixing your supports.

Setting the Barrel

You may choose to set your barrel into place at this point or you may wait until later. It depends on whether you are using an armature or a removable form.

Before building the barrel into the oven, we put a strip of ceramic wool around the front edge and secure it with a thin piece of wire. This serves as a fire-proof gasket that separates the metal barrel from where it touches the earthen or cement surround. We use this technique to help to reduce cracking from differential expansion.

Check for level!

Place a level in different directions on the baking shelves inside the Barrel Oven. You can also check with a speed level on the ridge of the door where it hinges. Check that the face of the oven lines up well with the front of the structure.

Place the barrel and make sure that the racks inside are level in all directions. You don't want to make slanted birthday cakes.

Building the Barrel Vault

You are now getting ready to build the arch over the barrel. One way to do this is by making an armature or form. Though we have often made our armature from metal, we have also used flexible branches/

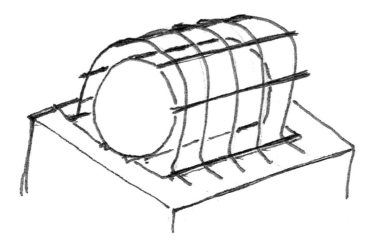

saplings which burn out during the initial firings. We have recently begun to use removable forms made from wood as we feel that the permanent metal arch form might be one cause of cracking we have observed. Whichever method you choose, be sure to maintain a consistent air space between the barrel and the bricks.

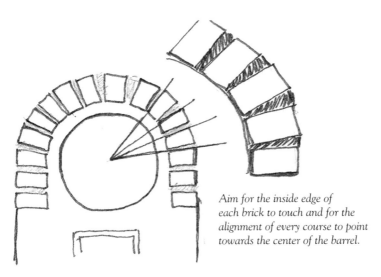

Aim for the inside edge of each brick to touch and for the alignment of every course to point towards the center of the barrel.

How to Make a Metal Arch Form:
We like to use ¼" pencil rod for the armature because it is both strong and flexible. Establish the length at which you will cut each one of your omega-shaped arch supports by using wire to mock it up first, making sure to include the two legs on either side. Remember, you are going for a 2" space all around the barrel. It is helpful to use the actual barrel to make your circular bends. Use wire to fasten 4-6 length-wise pieces which will hold all the arcs together. Make sure to place them so that they do not coincide with the chimney opening at the top. We then stretch expanded metal lath or chicken wire tightly over the framework, and tie it down with wire.

If you are using an armature, you will place it at least a few courses below the spring point so that it is well secured before the arch begins. The spring point is the height at which the arch starts on each side and is halfway up the barrel. This is where you will begin laying your mortar in a wedge shape between each course of bricks. The back wall of the oven should continue plumb and interlock as often as possible with the bricks on the arching sides.

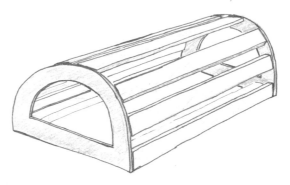

As mentioned, we have recently begun using a removable arch form. We cut two pieces of plywood which give the arch its shape and serve as the front and back faces of the form. We then connect the faces with pieces of wood that are the same length as the barrel. This shape is sometimes then covered with a membrane made of lath, mesh, melamine or cloth to create a solid skin which assists in laying the brick.

Make sure that the radius of your arch form is 2" (5 cm) greater than the radius of the barrel you are using to accomodate for the necessary air space. When placing the form, ensure that the top of the arch form corresponds to the height of the barrel sitting on its supports plus the additional 2" (5 cm) of air space. Anytime you are building with an arch form, place shims below the form so that you can later remove them and create space for the form to come out.

There is room for further development in these techniques. Eva recently built a Barrel Oven with a cob vault. Using sand forms, other methods of support and the Nubian vault are all promising directions.

Chimney

One of the last steps in construction is to place the chimney. Locate it at the top and center it along the length of the barrel (not the entire oven). While it is simplest to make a chimney out of pipe, it is also possible to build a masonry or cob chimney.

If using a metal armature, locate the chimney between arcs and snip a hole in the mesh the same diameter as your chimney. Cut and bend "flaps" into your metal pipe to serve as supports, insert, and build bricks around it. Check that your pipe is plumb.

If you are using a removable form to build your barrel vault, a slightly different approach to attaching the chimney is necessary. In this case, we have knotched the bricks that surround where the chimney will be placed so that the pipe has a stable seat. We then make sure to pack mortar around the pipe to secure it.

You can also install a damper in your chimney to keep more heat in the oven. An appropriate damper will correspond in size to the diameter of your chimney and can be purchased, found or made.

Refer to page 25 for additional information on chimney function and installation.

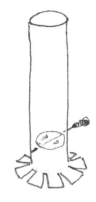

Cut flaps in the chimney pipe and secure with bricks and mortar around it. Make sure that your chimney is plumb and that you cut a hole in the mesh of your armature, if using one.

Details of notching brick to support the chimney when using a removable form. Bricks are carved with a grinder to form a seat for the pipe. Chimney and bricks are then mortared securely in place. (Both Photos, Aaron Maret)

The Seal

Upon building in the chimney, you have also completed the vault which now means that it is structurally sound on its own. If you have used a removable form, it is good to let your work set up at least overnight before removing it.

It is now time to place the barrel into the body of the oven, taking care that the oven shelves are level. We place a 4" wide strip of ceramic wool insulation between the barrel and the seal that surrounds it. Create this seal by filling in the space between the barrel and the arch with cob or carefully placed brick pieces joined together with mortar. A stiff mix can be made, for example, with 1 part clay and 3 parts sand. A mix rich in sand will help to prevent cracking. Build this mix in with care, making sure that it is compacted and that it adheres well to surrounding surfaces.

Your oven is now functional. It is best to let it dry out completely before using. If you are in a rush or in a wet climate you can make small curing fires that will help your oven dry faster. Make your first fires in the oven relatively small and gentle ones and build up over the course of a half dozen fires to full baking capacity so that your oven doesn't experience any initial shocks. It also helps to fire up your oven several times before applying finish plaster.

Once you are ready to bake in your oven, place a layer of clean, dry sand, 2-3" deep at the bottom of the oven to absorb and dissipate some of the direct heat from the flames. Even "dry" sand holds moisture which can cause rust inside your barrel. For this reason, it is best to add the sand upon making your first fires in the oven to fully dry the sand. You might choose to replace this sand after a few years of use.

Make sure that the seal is adhered well to surrounding surfaces. (Photo of two girls, Rachel Cox)

Finishing the Oven

There are many different options for how to plaster and decorate your oven including leaving it as it is. If you choose to give the oven a finishing touch, consider it a palette for color, texture and sculpture that will delight you. A finished plaster unifies and strengthens the surface as well as offering protection for the oven.

We have always plastered our ovens with an earthen plaster. Cement and lime-based plasters are also options.

Recipes for earthen plasters vary from place to place and depend greatly on the materials used. The color for your plaster will come from the beautiful natural colors of the clay and sand you use. Mineral pigments such as oxides and ochre can also be added.

Here is a general idea of a plaster recipe to try. We recommend making samples of varying proportions, letting them dry, and assessing what is best for your project. Keep in mind that you can change the finish over time.

Basic Earthen Plaster Recipe
1 part clay or clay-rich subsoil
2-3 parts sand
½ -1 part fiber (short chopped straw or manure)

Mix plaster ingredients well and apply with your hands or a trowel. Wet the oven surface thoroughly before applying plaster. This step ensures good adhesion. We find that two coats or more work best. Explore various textures.

If using an earthen plaster, you can make extra and save mix for future touch-ups and repairing cracks. Dry your plaster completely before storing by laying it out on a tarp or piece cardboard. You can then keep this dry mix in a bucket or bag and re-wet as needed.

Once you have built your oven you also have the opportunity to sculpt or carve shapes onto it. This can happen both before and/or after plastering. Sculptural designs can be simple, such as a few low-relief leaves here or there, and can also be more elaborate. How about turning your whole Barrel Oven into a mythical dragon or a rocket ship?! A basic earthen sculpting mix will be quite similar to your plaster mix though slightly dryer and often with longer fibers. Make sure to attach sculpture details well by pre-wetting the surface and working all materials together.

Other ideas for decorating include embedding stones, tiles or shells into your finished surface. Perhaps you are inspired by an intricate Moroccan style mosaic or maybe you have a special tile or gem stone that has meaning to you.

Remember that in addition to plastering, it is best to build a roof over your oven. It could be very simple like the image featured on the left.

For further reading on making and applying natural finishes, we highly recommend *Clay Culture* by Carole Crews and *Using Natural Finishes* by Adam Weismann and Katy Bryce.

Plastering is a fun activity that adds beauty and personality to your oven. Make a few samples and see what you like. (Photo/ oven with green roof, Pablo Perret and photo of tree roots with mosaic, Angela Francis)

Variations

The basic pattern that we have presented for the Barrel Oven is simple, and what we have the most experience with. There is a lot of room for experimentation and improvement. Here are some ideas:

Employing a "rocket-style" combustion chamber:

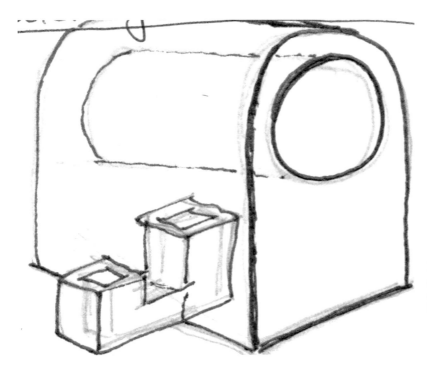

The "rocket-style" J-shaped combustion chamber offers a promising variaton for the Barrel Oven firebox.

Adapting the rocket firebox configuration from the book *Rocket Mass Heaters*, by Ianto Evans and Leslie Jackson, is a promising idea. Some important observations would include determining: the appropriate size firebox to create the right amount of heat; whether it is possible to vary the heat output for different baking needs as easily as in the basic design; whether or not the heat source is too concentrated and needs some sort of dispersion/ diversion to even out across the barrel.

Employing Baffles:

The idea to use baffles comes from Aprovecho Research Center's book *Capturing Heat Two*. In a similar oven design, it suggests using fiberglass batts

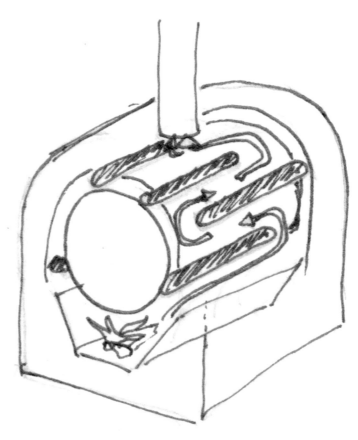

"Capturing Heat Two" is a great resource for learning more about fuel efficient cooking stoves and more.

covered with three layers of tinfoil to create the baffles. They could also probably be metal fins. Their design uses multiple metal barrels (cooking, spacer, insulator) which strikes us as complicated although it certainly would make experimenting with the placement and results of the baffles much easier than committing to an idea in masonry. Their book also recommends a very tight ¾"
(2 cm) spacing between the cooking barrel and the spacer which is intriguing as it seems very tight and may offer both great heat exchange, as well as potential draft problems.

Using Smaller Barrels and Other Metal Stock:

Sometimes the 55-gallon (200 L) barrel is just a little too big to cook in spontaneously for a small family. Max's brother's oven is made with a 26-gallon (100 L) barrel and is a wonderful size that has been used to cook for groups of 20 people and more. These smaller barrels are less prevalent, so keep your eye out and snatch one up if you see one.

We have a tall decommissioned propane tank that we have been saving to cut in two and make what we've fondly been calling a wood-fire microwave. The smaller propane tanks would probably work for this too. Larger diameter steel pipes could also be interesting. **It is essential to use extreme care when re-purposing any tank that may have contained combustible materials or residues.** It is recommended to unscrew the threaded valve and fill the tank with water to push out any combustible gases before cutting into it with anything that would cause sparks. The odor additive that is used in propane tanks can be very smelly when washed out, so take care to do so in an out-of-the-way place in order to create minimal environmental impact.

The wood-fired Barrel Oven is a pattern. You can use a range of different sized barrels, thick gauged pipe, or re-purpose other metal vessels. (Photo, Dylan Boye)

Fuel & Fire

Okay, it's time to use your Barrel Oven! Ideally, you've gathered wood for fuel and kindling of various sizes. One great advantage of the Barrel Oven is the variety of wood that you can use, including everything from cordwood down to orchard prunings, construction scraps and even broken-down fruit boxes. The wood can also be a variety of lengths up to the length of the firebox, including longer branches that don't fit into other stoves. In general, we use 1-5" (2-13 cm) diameter wood. Dry, seasoned wood is essential for a hot and efficient fire.

Start by making a robust paper and kindling fire to establish draft. If you have a damper, make sure it is open. Build the fire up by adding wood until you get a full fire along the length of the firebox. Experience and keeping track of the temperature inside the oven will be your best teacher in knowing how big to build the fire and how to maintain it.

Be aware of how the air flows into the firebox, through the fire, and how the smoke travels up and out. It is often helpful to close the firebox door slightly to reduce and focus the incoming air. You can use a piece of sheet metal or other suitable piece of metal as a substitute if you don't have a door.

Once you have a good fire going you can close your firebox door completely and leave the ash drawer open about ½" (1.3 cm). Experiment with letting different amounts of air in to see how the fire reacts. Remember that the door, the drawer and the damper are good tools for regulating the air flow.

Fire didn't go so well? Could be wet wood, wet weather, too little tinder, too much wind…. Try again. Fires have been made and used by people for cooking and heating since time immemorial.

Cooking In The Barrel Oven

You can bake, cook, roast, toast, warm, and dehydrate in a Barrel Oven! The possibilities are endless!

All types of pans and pots can be placed inside to cook food. Imagine your oven filled with cookie sheets with numerous treats, pizza stones with bubbling pies for your party, stock pots filled with soups and stews, and cast iron skillets baking your cornbread and your frittatas to perfection. How about the world's best Thanksgiving turkey... or three or four at a time... and pie pans with your favorite holiday creations!

Ceramic, glass and metal casserole dishes can also be filled with various meat and vegetable dishes, lasagna, enchiladas, shepherd's pie and more. Dutch ovens are well suited to the Barrel Oven for long, slow cooking, such as making roasts and stews.

We find that the Barrel Oven is hot and ready to bake in within 15-20 min of getting that good full fire going in the firebox. So what's ready? We find that it is generally at 350°- 400°F (176°- 204°C) at this point. This tends to be what we frequently bake at and what the majority of recipes call for. There are many oven thermometers that you can buy (usually under $10) which you can set inside the oven to read the temperature.

If you are looking for higher temperatures, say 500°- 700°F (260°- 371°C), the Barrel Oven can get there by making a hot blazing fire and maintaining it. This temperature is ideal for pizzas which cook best hot and fast.

Once your oven reaches the temperature you desire, you can keep a much smaller fire going to maintain the heat as you bake. Experiment with how small a fire you can make and keep going while maintaining the heat you desire. You will find that keeping the fire developed along the full length of the Barrel Oven will give you the best heat distribution throughout. In some situations you might want it hotter only in the back if say, you are cooking a variety of dishes within. Play with your Barrel Oven! You will find, depending on the materials that you use for construction, that your oven will require less and less fuel to maintain your cooking temperature. How sweet is that?! There will still be heat in the mass of the oven after the fire has gone out to keep on baking cookies and warming up those pies. As the temperature continues to drop you have a great opportunity to make crackers, "sun-dried" tomatoes, and even dry wood for your next fire.

As you get to know your oven, check in on the food you place inside. You might find that for certain dishes one area cooks faster than another. Different pans will behave in different ways. It won't be constant, perhaps just once per dish but pay attention and rotate, switch and pull your dishes as necessary.

Enjoy the versatility of your Barrel Oven. Parties and gatherings really showcase the Barrel Oven's majesty. They are a great tool for small and medium-sized farms and families alike!

COOKING IN THE BARREL OVEN:
Bake- Breads, meat, fish, vegetables, casseroles,
        desserts, pizza, soups, stews
Roast- Vegetables, fruit and meat
Toast- Bread, sandwiches, grains, nuts, cereals,
        coffee, granola
Warm- Leftovers **Melt-** Chocolate
Dehydrate- Fruits, herbs and vegetables

Recipes

Cooking in a Barrel Oven combines the familiar convenience many are accustomed to in gas and electric ovens with the unique enthusiasm that surrounds wood-fired cuisine. Any recipe you already make in another kind of oven can be made in a Barrel Oven. Try dishes that you already know and love and use what you have on hand to make creative combinations. Here we present some of our favorites from the Edleson kitchen to accompany you on your culinary journey.

CORNBREAD

You can successfully cook many moist cornbreads, frittatas and fruit cobblers in cast iron skillets. You will get best results by preheating the cast iron first, especially with a dish like cornbread which will get that nice crispy exterior. Serve this cornbread hot with your favorite chili or stew (which you can also make in your Barrel Oven!) Great for breakfast as well!

Ingredients

½ cup butter
½ - ¾ cup sugar
2 eggs
¼ - ½ tsp vanilla (adds romance)
1 cup milk or buttermilk
½ tsp baking soda
1 cup cornmeal
1 cup flour
½ tsp salt
Additions- grated cheese, chopped chilies, corn kernels, nuts, beans, etc.

Directions

- Heat Barrel Oven to around 375-400º F
- Place butter in a cast iron skillet or an 8" square pan. Then put pan in oven to melt butter while combining ingredients.
- Mix together dry ingredients in a bowl. Remove hot pan from oven and pour in most of the melted butter, leaving about a tablespoon to grease the pan well. Put skillet back in oven to keep hot.
- Add milk and eggs to bowl and stir just until blended. Pour batter into the prepared pan.
- Bake in the Barrel Oven for 30 to 40 minutes

Cornbread tastes great served with honey butter. Just mix room temperature butter with honey and voilà!

ROASTED VEGETABLES

It's easy to make large trays of seasonal roasted vegetables in your Barrel Oven!
Try combining a variety of colors and spices that will compliment your meal.

Have fun preparing your ingredients in various sizes. All vegetables taste good
together so play with what is fresh and on hand. Parsnips and fennel can give unique
variety and colorful bell peppers add lovely punctuation.

Ingredients

2-4 potatoes, try a nice mix of sweet and
  baking potatoes
1 small squash, like acorn
1 red or yellow onion
3-6 cloves of garlic, whole or chopped
1 TBS each of thyme, rosemary and or sage
¼ cup olive oil
2 TBS lemon or balsamic vinegar salt &
  pepper

Directions

- Preheat Barrel Oven to 475º F
- Cut all vegetables
- In a large bowl, combine ingredients
  and toss to coat evenly with oil and
  spices.
- Place vegetables in roasting pan.
- Roast for 35 to 40 minutes, stirring
  occasionally

MARY JANE'S PORK ADOBO

This delicious recipe comes from Max's mom who writes:

I started making Pork Adobo back in the Philippines in 1975, when I first met my dear husband Mark. Eating good local food was a big part of our courtship and happy marriage of the last 36 years!

Many consider Adobo to be the "national dish" of the Philippines, because it is so popular, and easy to prepare, with a long storage life (if you ever have leftovers!). Adobo is not limited to pork only, but you can also use chicken, seafood, meats or a vegetable medley.

After living more than 30 years in Indonesia, fresh ginger has snuck into my original Filipino recipe, which adds another layer of flavor. Indonesian "adobo" is called Babi Kecap, and was always the favorite meat dish of my sons, Max and Alex.

Cooking this recipe in a Barrel Oven superbly enriches the deep rich flavor of the sauce, creating a wonderful glazed meat that everyone will love.

Ingredients

3 lbs pork (shoulder, loin, belly) cut into
   2-inch pieces
8 cloves of peeled garlic, crushed
1 tbsp of finely chopped ginger
5 bay leaves
2/3 cup soy sauce
5 TBS brown sugar
1 TBS whole peppercorns
1/2 cup water
salt to taste
1/2 cup white vinegar

Preparation

- Preheat Barrel Oven to 350º F
- Combine all the above ingredients, except vinegar, in a cast iron or flame-proof casserole pot, and marinate for at least one hour. Make sure that all the meat is well covered with the marinade.
- Put the pot over a high heat stove top, and bring it to a boil for five minutes.
- Stir in the vinegar, and continue the cooking process in your Barrel Oven (pre-heated) until pork is tender, about one hour. Gently stir occasionally.

We like our Adobo a bit dry and glazed, so I remove the excess sauce from the cooking pot (when the meat is tender and almost finished), and reduce the sauce to half its volume on the stove top. Pour the reduced sauce back over the meat, and cook another 15 minutes in the oven.
Serve hot, with freshly steamed rice. Leftovers are fantastic in sandwiches or stir-frys.

- Boiling the pork initially on the stove top without vinegar makes the pork tenderize more quickly.

SQUASH & BLACK BEAN ENCHILADAS

Enchiladas always get hoots and hollers from the crowd. They can be filled with numerous ingredients and they are a great way to incorporate leftovers into a flavorful dish. This recipe blends the complimentary flavors and texture of squash and beans with traditional enchilada spices. Pre-roast the squash in your Barrel Oven with a bit of oil and salt for the best flavor.

Ingredients

1 squash (pumpkin, butternut or acorn),
pre-roasted or steamed
1 onion
1-2 cups cooked black beans
1 tsp cumin
1 tsp oregano
4 cloves of garlic, chopped
salt to taste
12 corn tortillas
Enchilada sauce, recipe next page
Grated cheese
Fresh cilantro for garnish

Directions

- Place a very small amount of oil in a skillet. Over med-high heat, cook corn tortillas for 15-30 seconds on each side. Place on plate for later.
- Chop onions and sauté with cumin and garlic in same skillet. Once onions are soft, add beans and oregano and cook for 10 min.
- Transfer ingredients in skillet to a bowl and mix with cooked squash
- Pour small amount of sauce in the bottom of baking dish
- Take one corn tortilla and place small amount of filling within, along with a small amount of grated cheese. Roll tortilla and place seam down in baking dish. Continue with all tortillas.
- Pour the rest of the enchilada sauce over the tortillas.
- Top with cheese and bake in the Barrel Oven for 30 to 40 minutes or until hot and bubbly
- Sprinkle with cilantro and serve with your favorite sour cream and salsa.

Make a nice hot fire for 15 minutes to bring your Barrel Oven up to baking temperature.

Delicious home made enchiladas baked in the Edleson's Barrel Oven. (Photo, Dylan Boye)

ENCHILADA SAUCE

The classic combination of chili and cocoa offer the palate a warm rich flavor. Add extra spice if you like it hot.

Ingredients
¼ cup veg oil
2 TBS flour
1 tsp cocoa powder
3 TBS chili powder
1 TBS cumin
1 tsp oregano
4 cloves of garlic, chopped fine
3 cups meat or vegetable broth
1 cup tomato paste
salt to taste

Directions
- Heat oil in skillet on med-high heat
- Add flour and stir to dissolve
- Add cocoa and chili powder and stir
- Slowly pour in broth, mixing frequently and add remaining ingredients.
- Cook over medium heat, stirring frequently for 5 minutes

PIZZA CRUST

Nothing makes a party happen like the promise of hot pizza coming out of a wood-fired oven. We like to make the dough ahead of time and then let our friends and family craft their own topping creations. Place pizzas directly on a hot pizza stone for the best and most authentic crust.

Ingredients:
1 cup warm water
2 tsp sugar or honey
2 tsp active dry yeast
3 TBS olive oil
1 tsp salt
2 ½ cups flour

Directions
- Combine the water, sugar and yeast together. Let sit for 5 minutes or until bubbly
- Add the olive oil and salt, then add flour and stir until the dough comes together into a solid, yet sticky ball
- Knead dough gently until smooth

- Let dough rise in a warm place for approximately ½ hour (or until dough doubles in size) in an oiled bowl with a wet cloth on top
- Split dough into 2-4 balls and roll, stretch or toss to form crust
- Place on pizza peel dusted with flour or cornmeal or an oiled pan
- Top with favorite toppings
- Slide into hot (400-500º F) Barrel Oven and cook pizza until hot and delicious!

Have fun exploring different sauces and fresh seasonal produce.

*Barrel Oven at the
Edlesons (Photo, Angela
Francis)*

FRIDAY NIGHT FISH

This is a quick and easy dish that is full of flavor. Lemon and oregano compliment the basic flavors of the fish and potatoes perfectly. Layer the ingredients beautifully, light some candles, and serve this dish with rice, warm baked bread and a fresh garden salad.

Ingredients:
5 TBS *olive oil*
3 TBS *lemon juice*
2 tsp *oregano*
Salt and pepper
1lb white fish fillets
2-3 onions, sliced very thin
4 cloves garlic, chopped finely
¼ cup chopped parsley
4-6 pre-cooked potatoes, sliced
4 sliced tomatoes
¾ cup stock or white wine

Directions
- Mix first four ingredients and marinate the fish in them for about 1 hour
- Place a layer of potatoes on the bottom of a baking dish. Add a little salt and pepper and then top with a layer of onions, fish, tomatoes, and garlic.
- Pour marinade and stock/white wine over all of the ingredients
- Bake at 400º F for about 15 min

Eva and BJ bake pizzas for a party in the Barrel Oven at the Ashevillage Institute. (Photo, Aaron Maret)

POLENTA PIZZA

This recipe comes to me from Janell Kapoor. She made it when I visited her at the Asheville Institute, a year after I led the building of their Barrel Oven. We wanted to celebrate so we invited a small group of friends to enjoy a polenta pizza brunch. This recipe is a fail-proof, fast, delicious, wheat-free option for pizza crust. It takes about two minutes to mix and ten minutes to bake. Janell recommends it for pizza, as well as wheat-free crackers and an option for lasagna. Needless to say, it was a hit!

Ingredients
1 cup polenta
1 cup water
1 raw egg
¼ cup olive oil
¼ cup hard cheese
Salt and spices to taste

Directions
- Mix all ingredients together.
- Pour into a baking dish about 1/3rd inch thick
- Cook in Barrel Oven at approximately 400º F for 10 minutes until the water has cooked off and the polenta is a thin crust.
- Remove from oven and top with your favorite pizza toppings. We used mozzarella, feta, eggplant, mushrooms and sundried tomatoes.
- Return dish to oven until it's ready, approximately another 10 minutes.

Serve with gusto and a fresh salad from the garden!

COUSIN LAINIE'S CHEDDAR BRUNCH BAKE

Eva's cousin Lainie adapted this recipe from *Gourmet Magazine's* "Ham and Cheddar Bread and Butter Pudding," December 1983. Enjoy this dish with loved ones on a leisurely weekend morning. Try layering in bits of various vegetables (peppers, mushrooms, olives,) and/or meat for an extraordinary brunch!

Ingredients

½ lb. sharp Cheddar, grated
2½ cups milk
12 slices homemade-type white bread,
crusts removed (best if it's a bit stale
¼ cup butter, softened
3 large eggs, beaten lightly
1 tsp dry mustard
Tabasco to taste

Directions

In a heavy saucepan melt the Cheddar in the milk over moderate heat, (or in your hot Barrel Oven,) stirring, then let the mixture cool. Cheese will sink to the bottom. Spread the bread with the butter and arrange 4 slices buttered side down in one layer in a buttered 8-inch-square baking pan. Make layers with the remaining bread.

In a bowl, combine the eggs, mustard, Tabasco, and a pinch of salt, and whisk in the Cheddar mixture. Ladle the mixture over the bread. Let the mixture stand, covered loosely, at room temperature for at least 1 hour or chilled overnight.

Preheat the Barrel Oven to 350º F. Put the baking pan in a large pan, and add enough hot water to the larger pan to reach halfway up the sides of the baking pan. Bake the pudding in the oven for 40 minutes. Serve warm.

MENU IDEA: Cousin Lainie's Cheddar Brunch Bake, Fruit Salad, Juice, Sausages, Croissants, Jam and Butter, Quick Bread (Persimmon, Banana, Cranberry), Coffee, Tea

We enjoy dreaming up what dishes we will make during the construction process. Here family members sculpt an apple tree on the back of their Barrel Oven.

The delicious carrot cake from our wedding sits amongst other tasty desserts. Enjoy cake with or without icing. (Photo, Marcie Stein)

CARROT CAKE

Max and I enjoyed this cake at our wedding. Moist and delicious, this cake is sure to please! Great as dessert, breakfast cake or a snack. We LOVE to make it with carrots from our garden and only ice it for the most special occassions.

Ingredients:

2 cups flour (white, wheat or mix)
2 tsp baking soda
1 tsp baking powder
1 tsp salt
1 ½ cups sugar
2 tsp cinnamon
1 cup vegetable oil
3 eggs
1 tsp vanilla extract
2 cups shredded carrots
½ cup chopped pineapple
½ cup raisins

Directions

- Mix the dry stuff, then add the wet stuff and mix all together.
- Put into cake pan
- Bake at 350º F for 45 min-1hr

Icing

1 cup cream cheese
¼ cup soft butter
1 ½ cups powdered sugar
Cream all ingredients together.
After icing, press chopped walnuts into sides of cake for a nice look,
added texture and delicious taste.

GLUTEN FREE PUMPKIN SPICE CAKE

Pumpkin adds amazing flavor and moisture to this delicious spice cake. The gluten free flour blend was described to me at a holiday potluck long ago. I have since used it as a wheat flour replacement in many dessert recipes. We like this recipe best in a bundt cake pan if one is available. Dust with powdered sugar for added festiveness.

Ingredients:
1 ¾ cup gluten free flour mix*
¼ tsp baking powder
1 tsp baking soda
½ tsp salt
½ tsp EACH nutmeg, cinnamon, cloves
1 ½ cups sugar
½ cup oil
1 cup pureed pumpkin
2 eggs

Directions
- Mix the wet stuff; mix the dry stuff separately.
- Add the dry stuff to the wet stuff and mix together.
- Put into a bundt pan, loaf pan, or muffin pan.
- Bake at 350º F for about 50 min. / 30 min. for muffins

You can use any GF flour mix. Here is one we like best for this recipe:

Gluten Free Flour Mix:
6 c. organic rice flour, 2 c. potato starch, 1 c. tapioca flour

Two friends slicing warm brownies to serve at a Barrel Oven party.

Frequently Asked Questions:

We have often found that the most important task is gathering materials. Once gathered, the materials answer many questions about design and process.

Doesn't the metal barrel burn out or rust away?
This question arises all the time. None of the barrels that we have built, used or heard about in our twelve years of observation of the Barrel Oven have ever burned out, or even shown wear enough to cause concern. We specifically asked about wear on the metal to the people we interviewed in research for this book to further develop our opinion.

We think this question arises from people's experiences observing metal burn barrels and barrels turned into stoves for heating. The former are obviously exposed to the extreme effects of weather along with fire which erodes them quickly and the latter are often under continuous use and under conditions of high temperatures and high oxidation.

Can a Barrel Oven be used for heating a space?

The question often arises whether the oven can also double as a heat source if placed inside a building. While there are many exciting possibilities for designing multi-functional fireplaces (often referred to as Masonry Heaters), the basic Barrel Oven design is focused on getting as much of the energy stored in the wood into cooking food, and therefore is not an efficient space heater. Ovens that are designed specifically for cooking often have lots of insulation to keep all the heat from your fuel stored and focused on cooking the food. There is potential, however, for applying the general principles of Barrel Oven design into wood-fired cooking and heating combinations.

Why are there not more Barrel Ovens?

The Barrel Oven could only become a folk pattern with the proliferation during the 20th century of metal barrels for the transport of lubricants, other petroleum bi-products and food. Also, many craftspeople focus their work on one material so artisanal ovens and stoves tend to be made entirely from either masonry or metal. We believe there are many possible interesting applications for mixing the two, and have also tried to share the challenges posed by their differing rates of expansion. We have found that these ovens are becoming more common in Argentina and Chile.

Can Barrel Ovens be made from insulative materials?

We have not yet experimented with building a Barrel Oven entirely from insulative materials such as insulative kiln brick or volcanic stone. We suppose that an insulative body might offer a lot of efficiency but also create an oven that fluctuates greatly in temperature, depending on the state of the fire. This can be challenging for baking. We do think that insulation around the thermal mass is a good idea.

"There is potential... for applying the general principals of Barrel Oven design into wood-fired cooking and heating combinations...."

Once the Barrel Oven is finished and the first pizzas are coming out, any worrying over small details gets carried away with the smoke up the chimney.

Troubleshooting

The crackled finish on this oven, built by Damian Colucci and Sylvia Gomez, was unexpected. What some may view as beauty, others may view as unacceptable.

We anticipate that this section will grow as this book gets into more hands and more Barrel Ovens are built. Please feel free to write emails to **barreloven@firespeaking.com** with questions you feel are not addressed in this text. Also, visit **www. handprintpress.com/barrel-oven** to stay updated about additions to the book.

Challenges, Room to Improve.... an Invitation!
We have built about ten Barrel Ovens and eaten from a handful of others that friends have built. These experiences with the oven and with the food they produce were more than convincing enough for us to feel that it would be worthwhile getting

information out about the Barrel Oven to more people. We are certain that there is significant room for improvement and we hope you will consider this book an invitation to collectively improve all of our knowledge on the subject.

Areas that we feel need work and are in need of improvement include:

- Finding the easiest and best ways to build the "vault" around the barrel.
- Experimenting with different firebox and flue path configurations to further improve combustion, heat exchange into the barrel and evenness of heating.
- Cracks often develop on the plastered surface of the Barrel Ovens we have built. We think that this is due to the expansion and contraction of various parts of the oven. It could also be due to a potential vulnerability in the vaulted shape of the oven when exposed to expansion stress in heating cycles. Especially for outdoor ovens, considering surface cracks as beautiful natural occurrences is likely the best way to fix them. We have had some success persistently filling cracks while the oven is hot (most expanded). This seems to reduce and sometimes eliminate cracking. One colleague told us that he actually sticks dimes in the cracks to hold them in their open state and then re-plasters. Covering the oven in lath or mesh and applying a hard (cement or lime) plaster may be a solution although we have not yet tried this. Another possible approach we are looking forward to trying, despite the added complexity, is adapting the idea of "double-skin" construction from modern masonry heater and brick oven building. This technique involves building two distinct masonry walls with an expansion joint in between so that any cracks on the inside "core" don't surface/ show themselves on the exterior. One reason for publishing this book is to develop a broader base of common experience upon which we can accelerate improvements such as solving this challenge.

There are so many solutions. Use what you have and be creative.

Bibliography

References:
These are links to the original information in Spanish that we began working from:
ArtePan www.artepan.com.ar
Canelo de Nos www.elcanelo.cl/horno-mixto.html

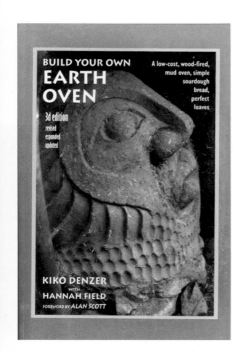

Related Reading:
Here is a list of books about ovens, use of fire and basic design of space that we recommend to further your investigation:

Build Your Own Earth Oven, by Kiko Denzer
The Book of Masonry Stoves, by David Lyle
The Bread Builders, by Alan Scott
Rocket Mass Heaters, by Ianto Evans, Leslie Jackson
The Pattern Language, by Christopher Alexander

DVD:
Mud, Hands, A House (Jorge Belanko, Gustavo Marangoni, Daniel Lugones)
This is the best DVD on natural building available. Includes assessing and making mixes, many different wall systems, and all of the steps of building a building. Very hands-on and practical.
Learn to make adobe bricks, straw-clay, clay-based plasters and paints, wattle and daub and more!
www.firespeaking.com/dvd

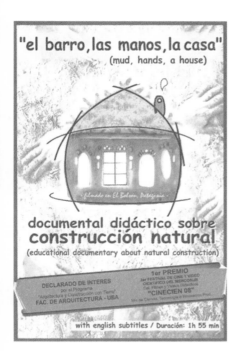

Websites:
Firespeaking www.firespeaking.com
Handprint Press www.handprintpress.com
Masonry Heater Association of North America www.mha-net.org

Appendix I: Sample Material Lists

Manos En La Tierra Barrel Oven	Ashvillage Institute Barrel Oven	Dabbeni Family Barrel Oven
Oven Recycled oil drum, hinges, old bed-spring, ingenuity	**Oven** 1 Firespeaking Barrel Oven Kit	**Oven Kit** 1 Firespeaking Barrel Oven Kit
Foundation & Pad On-site stone	**Foundation & Pad** ¼ yard of 1 ½" round fill rock Recycled Cinder Block and Local Stone 12 Full Cinder Blocks 16x8x8 4 Half Cinder Blocks 8x8x8 10 Red Brick	**Foundation & Pad** 8 Gravel 5gal ea 2 1x4x8' Form Boards 9 Block 8x8x16 4 Block 8x8x8 3 Block 4x8x16 1 Mortar Mix 80# 16 Dobies 4 Concrete Mix 90# 2 Rebar" x 20' 10 Solid Bricks 2.5"
Oven Body On-site stone	**Oven Body** 140 Compressed Earth Blocks 2 Firebrick	**Oven Body** 280 Cored Bricks 36 Solid Bricks 2.25"
Earthen Mortar On-site clay-rich earth, sifted	**Earthen Mortar** ½ yard clay ½ yard sand	**Earthen Mortar** 4 Fireclay 50# (5gal ea) ½ yard sand
Armature Young flexible branches from nearby tree	**Metal for Armature** 6 10" lengths of ¼" pencil rod 1 Spool of Tie Wire (16 gauge) 1 4x8 Sheet of Diamond Lath	**Metal for Armature** 6 Pencil Rod 10' 1 Metal Lath
Lintels Various recycled metal and brick	**Angle Iron, Lintels** 1 18" of 2" x $^3/_{16}$" L Iron 2 44" of 1½" x $^3/_{16}$" L Iron	**Angle Iron, Lintels** 1 10' of 1½" x $^3/_{16}$" L Iron 1 17" of 2" x $^3/_{16}$" L Iron 1 Stove Gasket
Chimney On-site stone and "ready mix" earthen mortar	**Chimney** 1, Stove Pipe 5 x 60 1, 5" Chimney Top 1, 5" Cast Iron Damper 1, Storm Collar for 5" Pipe	**Chimney** 1 China Top 6" 1 Cast Iron Damper 3 Stove Pipe 6 x 24 1 High Temp Silicone 1 Stove Paint Black 1 Chimney Flashing 1 Storm Collar 1 Trim Plate
	Plaster 4 Local Red Clay (5gal ea) 8 Sand (5gal ea) 2 Chopped Straw (5gal ea) 2 final coats of "Glue Coat" made of 1 part Elmers glue and 4 parts water	**Plaster & Tile** 4 Local Brown Clay (5gal ea) 10 Sand (5gal ea) 3 Chopped Straw (5gal ea) 6 Tile 16" x 16" 1 Sanded Grout 1 Versabond Mortar *Tile was added to the oven's base.*

Appendix 2:
Obtaining a Barrel Oven Kit

Eventually we hope to provide a list of people around the world who make Barrel Oven kits as a cottage industry. This is one of our reasons for enthusiasm about the Barrel Oven: its potential to provide meaningful and productive activity for many people in their local communities. It is a great project for high school and community-college metalworking classes. We hope that the proceeds of selling this book can help to support us in putting together a manual that more specifically addresses the metal work involved.

Barrel Oven Kits from Firespeaking:

The Barrel Oven Kit that we produce is a synthesis of about ten years of collaborative effort by metal-smiths and natural builders to refine a basic set of metal components that allows you to build a Barrel Oven simply and to use it productively and with ease over many years. The photo below shows all the parts included in a whole "kit." You also have the option to only purchase the "barrel." We are very proud to make these components as part of our home/farm economy.

See **www.firespeaking.com/barrel-oven** for a current price list and availability.

The Barrel Oven from Friespeaking includes the barrel, an insulated door with custom hinges and two oven racks. The "kit" option includes a firebox door, ash grate and ash drawer which doubles as an air register. (Photo of Max w/ grinder, Dylan Boye)

Appendix 3: Personal Stories

The Barrel Oven at Valle Pintado *by Alex Edleson*

The Barrel Oven has been nothing less than a pillar in my life. Week to week we bake bread in our beloved oven and this cycle weaves a tapestry of warmth into our community. Our oven has withstood the test of time and has wooed the hearts of many volunteers who have come to work, and those of

visitors who flow through our community farm in Patagonia, Argentina. It is dear to my heart, and might I also say in my brother Max's: this oven was Max's first – to think the first that lit that fire of passion that now has spread like wildfire into the homes of many… this is the story of an oven for the many, but unique to each.

The story of our first Barrel Oven begins in a barn in rural Buenos Aires. On a visit to our good friend and farmer Damian, we noticed an old metal drum tossed in the corner of his barn. We had seen and participated in the building of Barrel Ovens before, but it was now time to design our own. We wanted to build it to give life to the shack that we inherited

*The Barrel Oven at Valle
Pintado has been used by friends
and family for over seven years.*

on the land near the town of El Bolsón, in Patagonia, where we had recently acquired land. But in our experience, it had seemed that the classic 200 liter (55 gal.) barrel was a little too big for our needs and for the space we had. We barely remembered ever having seen these smaller 120 liter (33 gal.) drums as we had found that day at Damian's barn. It seemed to have served a pharmaceutical company once upon a time, and now would be the remedy for our needs.

The long 24-hour bus trip back to Patagonia allowed us plenty of time to ponder the wonders we would create in this oven. In the mean time, while we waited for bus connections in the terminals, other people to my dismay would mistake it for a trash can! Little did they know...

Since its destiny would eventually be a community oven, it was birthed collectively by a group from the local institute for teacher training, who had come to do their retreat with us on our land. Given that our shack was so small, we decided to build the face (or door) of the oven inside and have the ass (or body) sticking out, so that we would not lose valuable interior space.

From that day on, the Barrel Oven would forge masterpiece after masterpiece on our farm – blackberry crumbles in the fall, roasted potatoes in the winter, and the occasional trout caught in our river. Everything was great, until one day the whole building burned to the ground....

We were all asleep the night it happened. It appears that a faulty chimney pipe on the earthen water heater I had recently added to the community shack had possible ignited the super dry wood of the old beams of the shed. Volcanoes among our Andean range had been active as of late, so even though tremendous explosions shook the earth, I mistook them as regular seismic activity from the volcano and I just rolled in my bed and didn't even go to check it out. When a neighbor finally came around to let me know that the shack had disintegrated in flames, I pulled myself together to witness the horror, drawing upon the best of Buddhist attitudes of acceptance....

As the smoke cleared, very little was left intact, but not all was lost. In one corner, wholesome and solid as ever, was our beloved Barrel Oven, still standing like the corner stone of our community building. I was not worried, it could be rebuilt...

And so it was that the community kitchen was rebuilt... this time three times bigger. Many people came together in the effort to piece together the new kitchen and in doing so, the old oven was a key

The Barrel Oven which Alex and Max built... in the original shack. (Photo, Max Edleson)

coordinate in assembling the new design. I wonder how many buildings are designed around an oven?

And today, seven years after it was built, the oven is a solid hearth that gives life to our community. Among our weekly rituals with the many volunteers that come to work and share life with us on the farm, is "oven night." There has to be at least one day in the week when we bake our weekly bread, but of course, if we are going to fire the beast up we are going to make the most of the fire. A batch of bread is followed by a quiche for dinner that surfs on the heat that follows; someone else slips in a pie as the heat surges on; and even though the fire has died, someone else hands in a tray of thin apple slices to dehydrate, riding on the gentle heat of afterward.

Our Barrel Oven has grown with us and I give thanks for the nourishment it has provided our community space. It unites many of the principles of sustainable living that we believe in: living with local materials, recycling the old, and using our hands to build and shape *our* spaces and give life to our imagination. Creativity is like bread: imagine it, knead it, mold it, and let the heat of passion manifest your dreams!

The Barrel Oven feeds many volunteers weekly at Granja Valle Pintado CSA farm. (Photo of oven, Alex Edleson)

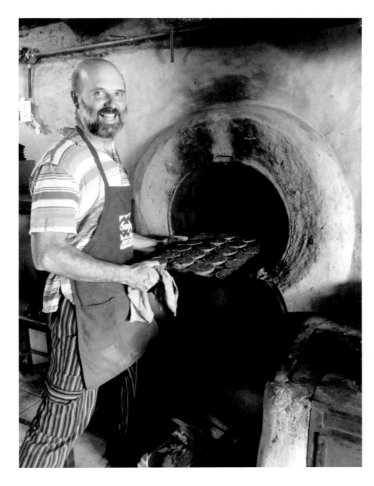

Daniel is the head cook at CIDEP, a permaculture center in Argentina. He has used this oven for over five years. (Photo, Gabriel Kaufmann)

Daniel Batista, El Bolsón, Argentina (8/1/2011)

What do you like about the Barrel Oven?

Using wood as a fuel connects with the forest, with the earth, and with the nature around me. I like the smells that surround the fires I make. I like to see the fire. I can use all kinds of branches, large or small, in my oven - whatever I've got! The Barrel Oven that we have in our house is a big one so I know when we light it that we are cooking for a lot of people, for groups.

How often do you use the Barrel Oven?

At CIDEP, our educational [permaculture] center we use the Barrel Oven throughout our summer season when we are receiving visitors, volunteers and workshop participants. For about four months of the year, from December to March (Daniel lives in Patagonia, Argentina, in the southern hemisphere where the seasons are the opposite of the northern hemisphere's). During those months, we are usually an average of 40 people who are eating here on a daily basis. We do not use the oven every day except in weeks that we have received up to 150 people at one time. When we are 30 or 40 people, we use the oven every other day and make an effort to cook a number of things at once. For example, if we are baking stuffed zucchini for a meal, we'll make sure

The Barrel Oven helps to celebrate the passage of time! (Photo, CIDEP)

to bake a round of bread and make some kind of healthy dessert as well. We're able to bake bread with a lively fire. When we take that bread out of the oven, we take advantage of the more stable and moderate temperature of the oven to do our dessert baking.

How would you improve the oven that you are using?

I would install an oven thermometer so I could monitor the temperature inside the oven better.

The Barrel Oven at CIDEP frequently feeds gatherings of up to 150 people. (Photo, CIDEP)

How has your oven fared over time? How long have you been using the Barrel Oven? Has the bottom of the barrel shown signs of wear? Have you had to replace the barrel?

The Barrel Oven that we are using on the farm at this moment is five years old and we have not had to change the barrel out. The barrel for our oven was originally used for transporting honey and therefore has a fairly thick wall.

What do you think are the strengths and weaknesses of this style of oven compared with other kinds of wood-fired ovens? compared with gas or electric ovens?

In all my cooking experience, I have not come across a single oven that cooks completely evenly - whether it be a gas or a wood-fired one. To help with the evenness of the heat in our oven, we placed sand in the bottom portion of the barrel so that the intensity of the heat from the fire does not directly reach the food.

We have a system of rotating our pans... a quarter of the way through we turn the pans around on the same shelf that they sit on because the back of the oven cooks faster than the front. Our oven has an

This Barrel Oven is conveniently built with its face in the plane of the kitchen wall. Notice the door which provides access to wood storage outside.

"Putting a plate of food on the table has great significance. There are many stories that come together on the table....Having a wood-fired oven in this context is like having a wonderful accomplice - a perfect ally...."

upper and a lower shelf so about half-way through the cooking process, we then switch the "goods" on the top with the "goods" on the bottom.

Three strengths of the oven: It is...

Economical: It uses all kinds of different local wood sources (prunings, cordwood, scraps, etc.) and you can cook a number of things at the same time.

Ecological: We live in a forest, we gather the dry wood that the forest offers us. To cook with gas, on the other hand, we have to bring in gas and tanks from another location, pay for their contents and for their transportation.

(Energetically) Inspiring: It is pleasant to be with the fire, to feed it, and to see it amidst our clay walls.

What's the favorite dish you make in your Barrel Oven?
Bread, Pizza and Casseroles. Desserts require the most special attention since they demand a moderate fire and more even heat.

Do you have any special advice or recommendations to someone thinking about building themselves a Barrel Oven? or to someone thinking about using the Barrel Oven for a catering or baking business?
Suggestions for construction:
Make sure you think about where and how you install the chimney.

Reinforce the bottom of the barrel where the fire hits it directly with an additional sheet of metal.

Place sand in the bottom portion of the inside of the barrel.

Make sure the oven door, damper and firebox door are well-constructed.

Suggestions for someone thinking about using a Barrel Oven:

It is helpful to have a second oven to use as an alternative when you only need to cook a small amount of food.

Any other thoughts about your experience and relationship with the Barrel Oven?

[As the head cook at an educational center], using this oven has always gone hand in hand with cooking and baking with people who are on a path of learning a new way of living, a new way of doing things, a new way of sharing with others, and a new definition of nutrition. They are looking for something wholesome that makes sense. I have watched this oven accompany them in their apprenticeship and growth.

Putting a plate of food on the table has great significance. There are many stories that come together on the table. It's like theater. There is a script, intention, rehearsals, the collection of raw ingredients, the tools, the spices. To have it all, to bring it all together, and then in a single instant bring it out on to the stage. Having a wood-fired oven in this context is like having a wonderful accomplice - a perfect ally.

Seeds and plants form the basis of our diet. We avoid meat and dairy products. We feel strongly that these guidelines provide for an energy-filled, healthy and sustainable diet.

Daniel, head cook, rolls out dough and makes loaves of bread to be cooked in the Barrel Oven. (Photo, CIDEP)

Jorge Belanko, Nora's husband, shows a Barrel Oven he built with students at an adult vocational school. (Photos, Nora Belanko)

Nora Belanko, El Bolsón, Argentina (8/8/2011)

What do you like about the Barrel Oven? What do you not like about the Barrel Oven?

I like the speed with which one can begin cooking and the little wood necessary for cooking. It is also ideal for extended baking sessions where one is cooking large quantities because the effect of the heated outside walls of the oven begins to kick in - like with the traditional dome oven. I don't like its size for two people. For this purpose, I would make one with a smaller 100 Lt. (28 gal.) drum or perhaps with half the length of a full-sized drum.

How would you improve the oven that you are using?

To make it even easier to use, I would improve our oven by installing an oven thermometer on the door of the oven in order to make sure that the temperature in the oven was neither too high nor too low. It is ideal, anyways, to have a double-walled door that includes a refractory insulation between the two walls to keep more of the heat more even inside the oven.

How has your oven fared over time? How long have you been using the Barrel Oven? Has the bottom of the barrel shown signs of wear? Have you had to replace the barrel?

Describe your use of the Barrel Oven. How often do you use the Barrel Oven? Do you notice that some parts of the oven are hotter than others? Which ones? Do you have ideas about how to even this out?

We built our oven in 1996. The oven was used three days a week for at least eight years and also went through a period of six months where we were baking bread and pizza shells (about 90 lbs. of bread and 50 pizza shells) every day. One of our neighbors has also used the oven to cook whole pigs or sheep once a year.

The barrel has not burned out. In fact, the bottom still seems to be in quite good shape. We used one of those honey barrels. We also placed a layer of sand on the bottom so that the heat would even out better.

What do you think are the strengths and weaknesses of this style of oven compared with other kinds of wood-fired ovens? compared with gas or electric ovens?

The strength of this kind of oven is its efficiency in terms of the amount of wood required, the cleanliness of the process and the speed in cooking. It begins to cook practically once you've lit your fire. We use half of a kilo of wood for each kilo of bread that we bake. You can use a wide range of combustibles for your fuel including cordwood, branches, leaves, dried manure, paper, etc., given that the fire and the smoke doesn't have direct contact with the food.

"...The oven was used three days a week for at least 8 years and also went through a period of 6 months where we were baking bread and pizza shells..."

Baking lots of delicious bread for sale in the Belanko's Barrel Oven.

What's the favorite dish you make in your Barrel Oven?
Everything comes out well for us in this oven!

Do you have any special advice or recommendations to someone thinking about building themselves a Barrel Oven? or to someone thinking about using the Barrel Oven for a catering or baking business?
My advice is that you build yourself one and that you use it as a form of efficiently using a locally available fuel source and preventing the overutilization of firewood and other forms of environmental pollution.

This oven is ideal for family-scale or small cooperative enterprises. It is easy to use - even children can use it.

Any other thoughts about your experience and relationship with the Barrel Oven?
About the cracks that result from the oven's expansion upon heating up.... We used a tube of high temperature silicon on our daughter Natalia's oven. We ran a thick bead between the drum and the mud surrounding it and it has held up quite well.

Freshly baked loaves of bread from Nora Belankos's wood-fired Barrel Oven.

Alexia Allen, Woodinville, WA (8/8/2011)

Alexia is a naturalist and dedicated teacher of wilderness awareness skills. Here she lights a celebratory friction fire in her Barrel Oven by traditional hand drill method.

What do you like about the Barrel Oven?
That it is a heart and gathering place of the farm. It is efficient and beautiful and provides a wonderful way to feed groups of people both large and small. It is fun to use and all things considered is holding up well. It burns cleanly, and uses wood that is too long for my woodstove inside.

What do you not like about the Barrel Oven?
I see some of the bricks deteriorating with frequent use, so I worry about its longevity. I am also glad I did not personally have to make all the adobe bricks for it. The front of the oven is significantly cooler than the back, so I sometimes have to turn pizzas around, or they get charred on one side and not done enough on the other.

How would you improve the oven that you are using?
Metal rails for the ash tray so that I do not crumble the bricks as much when I take the tray in and out. A more rust-resistant finish on the metal parts.

The Barrel Oven offers surprising convenience because it is hot and ready to bake in within 15-20 minutes of lighting a fire.

How has your oven fared over time? How long have you been using the Barrel Oven? Has the bottom of the barrel shown signs of wear? Have you had to replace the barrel?

The bottom of the barrel gets red-hot when the oven is really fired up. I haven't replaced the barrel. I can now see gaps in the plaster where it meets the barrel.

How often do you use the Barrel Oven?

At least once a month–it's been the core of monthly pizza potlucks at Hawthorn Farm. I also use it for other special occasions, probably twice a month on average. I don't usually cook in there unless its for a crowd of people. My favorite feast was cooking pizza for 70 people!

What do you think are the strengths and weaknesses of this style of oven compared with

other kinds of wood-fired ovens compared with gas or electric ovens?

It heats up quickly, can cook for a huge number of people and stay hot. Latecomers to the party can throw a few more sticks in the firebox and heat the oven back up to pizza temperature.

What's the favorite dish you make in your Barrel Oven?

PIZZA PIZZA PIZZA. That's really what I have made successfully. Fortunately pizza doesn't get old.

Do you have any special advice or recommendations to someone thinking about building themselves a Barrel Oven? or to someone thinking about using the Barrel Oven for a catering or baking business?

Have Max and Eva build it for you, that's my recommendation. I can feel the love and attention in the oven, and that is a significant part of the story, the good memories of the group who made it. As far as baking/cooking in there, practice practice practice. It's an art. I would love to offer use of my oven to someone doing commercial baking, and have contemplated it myself (though I lack the temperament to be a baker). Anyone in the northeast Seattle area want to try?

Editors' note: This was the first Barrel Oven that we built in North America. The adobe bricks that were made were very silty and degraded over time. Alexia has since rebuilt her oven anew. This experience has also led us to paint all exposed metal parts with high temperature stove paint.

"...It heats up quickly, can cook for a huge number of people and stay hot. Latecomers to the party can throw a few more sticks in the firebox and heat the oven back up to pizza temperature..."

Paolo and Astrid Dabbeni, Portland, OR (1/19/2011)

What do you like about the barrel oven?
Paolo: It is outdoors and uses wood; it is made of earth and was made by us and friends.
Astrid: The opportunity to learn about community building.

What do you not like about the barrel oven?
Paolo: Nothing yet.
Astrid: When you burn a "batch of cookies" you are burning 4 cookie sheets not just two…hahaha!

Why did you decide to build a barrel oven?
Paolo: Astrid has been wanting a pizza oven for a long time and for her 40th (oops 41st) birthday we decided it was what she wanted.
Astrid: I wanted something special for my birthday to represent family, community and friends that would be more than just a one-time event. Heat, warmth, food and gathering together to create all came to mind when we decided on a outdoor oven. We also really struggled with whether to go with a more traditional pizza oven and the barrel oven. The final deciding factor was the time it took to fire up and preheat.

How often do you use the barrel oven?

Paolo: We probably have used it twice a month more or less.

Astrid: Definitely more than less! Since we have had the oven ready to fire that first night two months ago, we have fired it up at least 8+ times (my bday, cycle cross party, Thanksgiving dinner, Ricks family, cookie bake, Miguel's dad, new year's eve, Maya's bday…!) LOL

Do you notice that some parts of the oven are hotter than others? Which ones? Do you have ideas about how to even this out?

Paolo: So the back seems hotter and the top also. So I would have the racks a bit lower so that the top is not so close and build the oven so that the back of the barrel is in contact with the bricks so it does not heat as much.

What do you think are the strengths and weaknesses of this style of oven compared with other kinds of wood-fired ovens?

Paolo: It warms up fast and it stays warm, it gets to 350 F in 15 min., it is very clean and you don't have to worry about spilling, the sand at the bottom works great. You can burn any type of wood and even yard debris and less than dry wood.

Astrid: It is so easy to start a fire and keep it burning. Makes me feel like a master-fire starter :).

Compared with gas or electric ovens?
Paolo: Being outside it doesn't matter if you burn stuff or make smell, you can cook 4 large pizzas at one time. !!!

What's the favorite dish you make in your barrel oven?
Paolo: Pizza but we have also done turkey for Thanksgiving with yams and stuffing both inside and outside the bird, potatoes, pork roasts, cookies.

Do you have any special advice or recommendations to someone thinking about building themselves a barrel oven? or to someone thinking about using the barrel oven for a catering or baking business?
Paolo: The building party was great, it is the best feeling remembering the moments and the people that build it with us while using it. As we saw the first night that we used it with Eva you can cook a lot of pizzas in a short time...
Astrid: Could not agree more...the memories of creating this amazing oven will always be with me

(Photo of the Dabbeni family oven, June Bonnheim)

(Group photo of Barrel Oven builders Jennifer Cvitanich)

and everyone who helped. A sense of ownership with everyone who helped make the oven is such a good feeling. I LOVED hearing Zio Miguel tell his dad with such pride that he helped make this oven!

Any other thoughts about your experience and relationship with the barrel oven?

Paolo: It is great to have a covered area on top of the oven, for rain and wind. The tables on the side are also very useful for loading and unloading the oven and to move the pizzas around. Still trying to figure out the best way to store the wood near the oven.

Astrid: Our teachers and support leaders were instrumental in making this such a successful experience. A book would have been nice to have read beforehand but in no way would it have been able to replace what Eva, Max and Casey brought to this experience.

Vistara Barrel Oven - Step by Step Photos

Throughout the book we have emphasized that your project will be unique to your location and the materials that are available to you. Here is one example of a Barrel Oven construction sequence built with homemade adobe bricks.

1. Homemade adobe bricks

2. Rubble trench foundation

3. Urbanite Pad

4. Layout

5. Build base

6. Base, Grate and Door

7. Bricks, Firebox, Lintels

8. Bricks, Firebox, Lintels

9. Set Barrel

10. Armature, More Bricks

11. Begin Arch, Ceramic Wool

12. More Bricks

13. Chimney

14. The Seal

15. Shaping and Rough Plaster

16. Make sure to bake some cookies!

17. Finish Plaster and Pizza Party
ENJOY!